A, B, C for Toddler Engineers

Jie Jacquot, Ph.D.

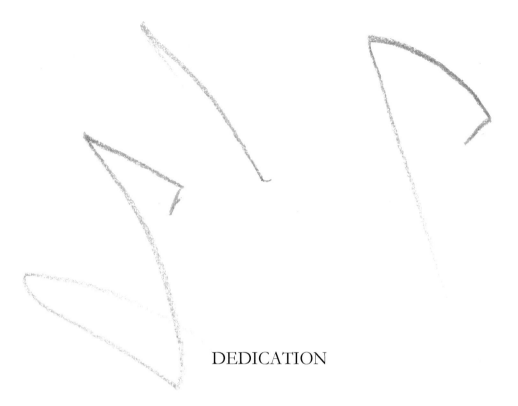

DEDICATION

To my beautiful little angel, Skyler, who is no doubt already a brilliant engineer in training.

Jie Jacquot

ACKNOWLEDGMENTS

Thanks go out to my parents and husband, who make it all possible.

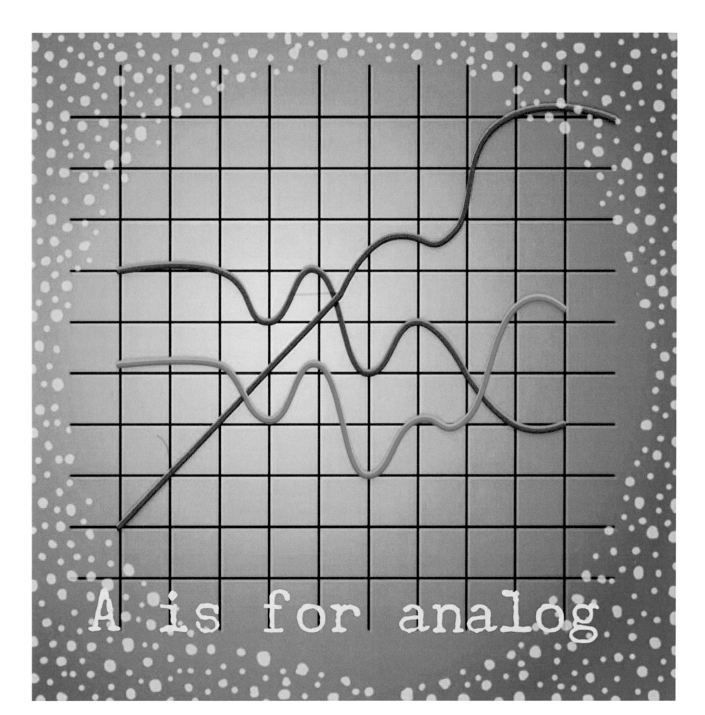

A is for analog

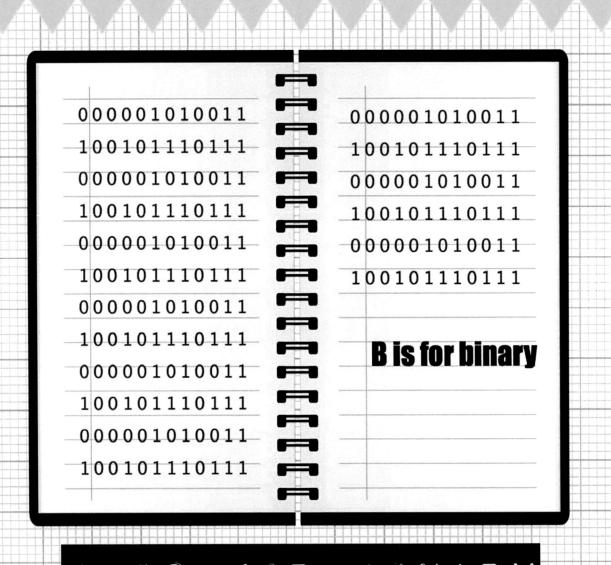

B IS FOR BINARY

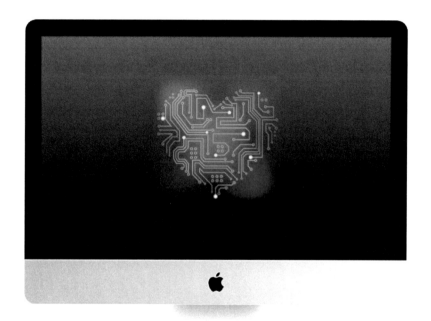

C is for circuit

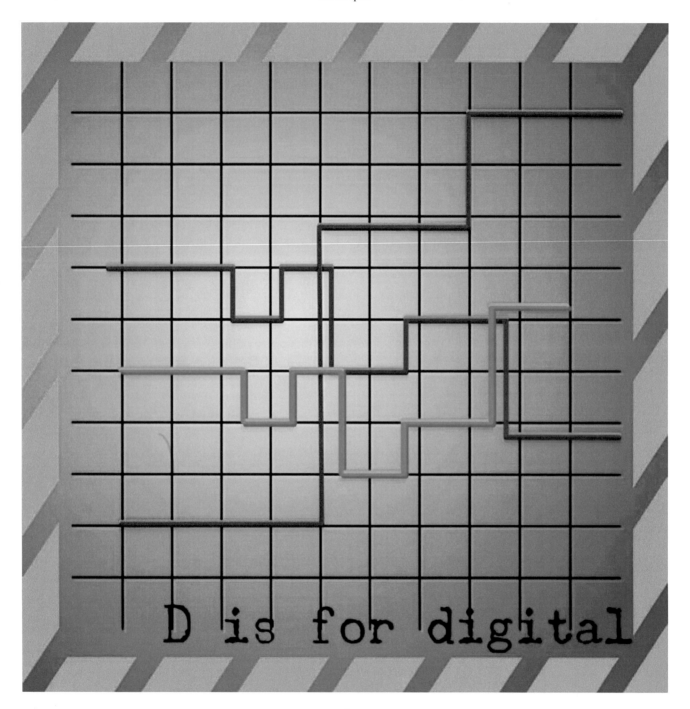

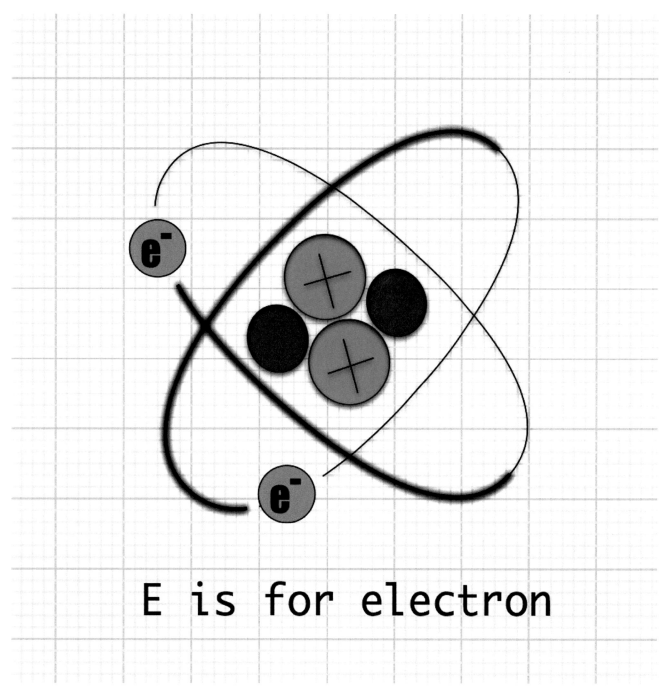

E is for electron

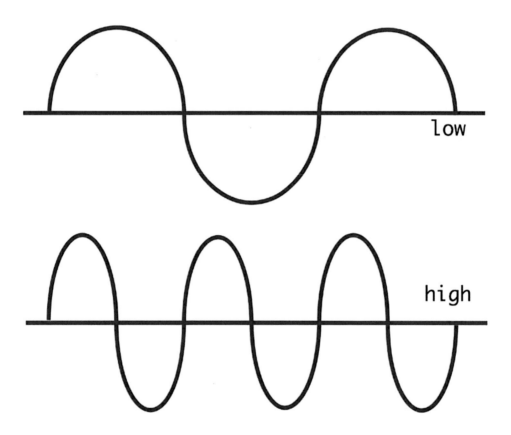

F is for frequency

G is for ground

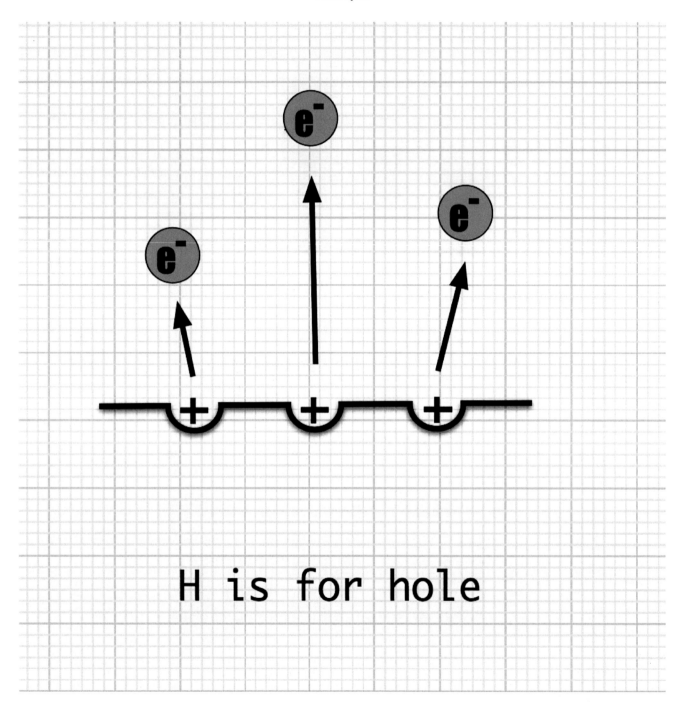

H is for hole

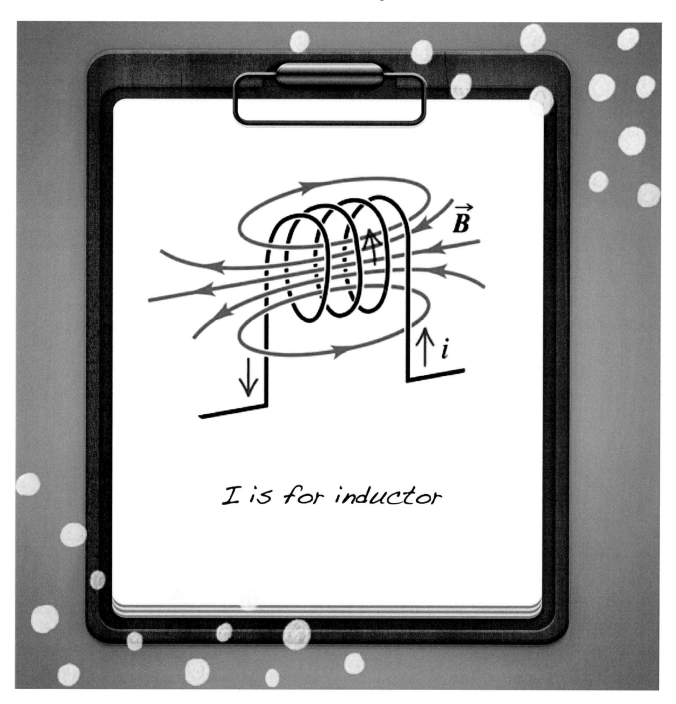

I is for inductor

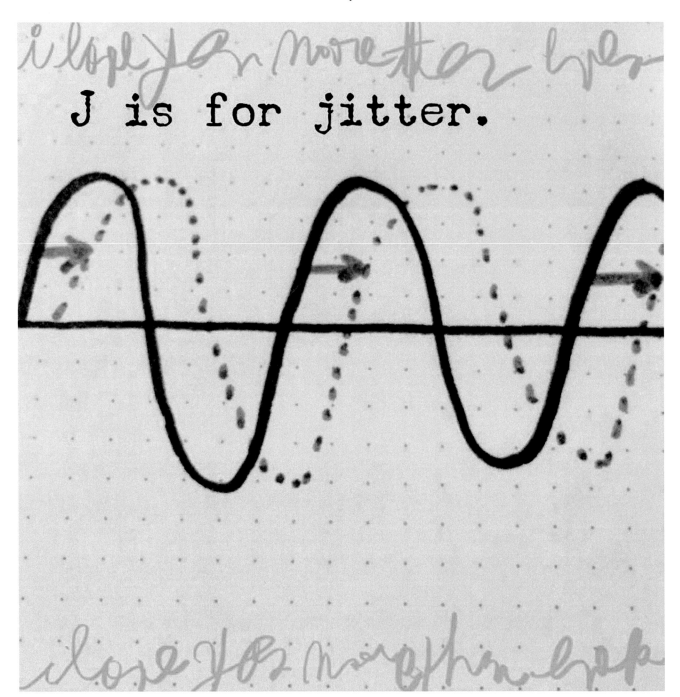

J is for jitter.

K is for key

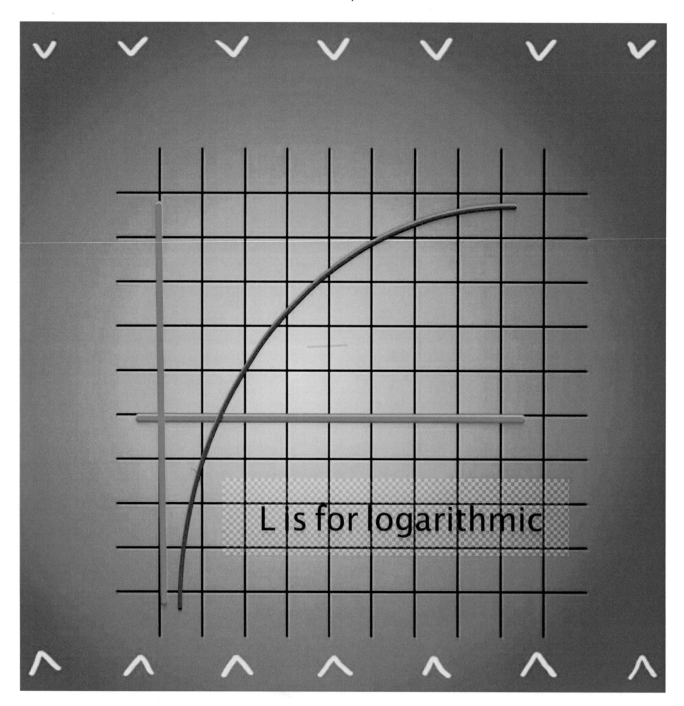

L is for logarithmic

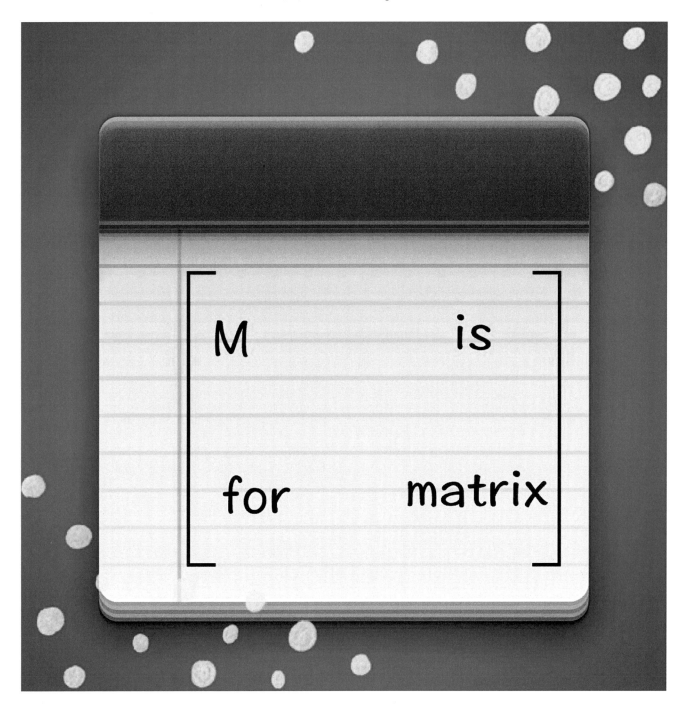

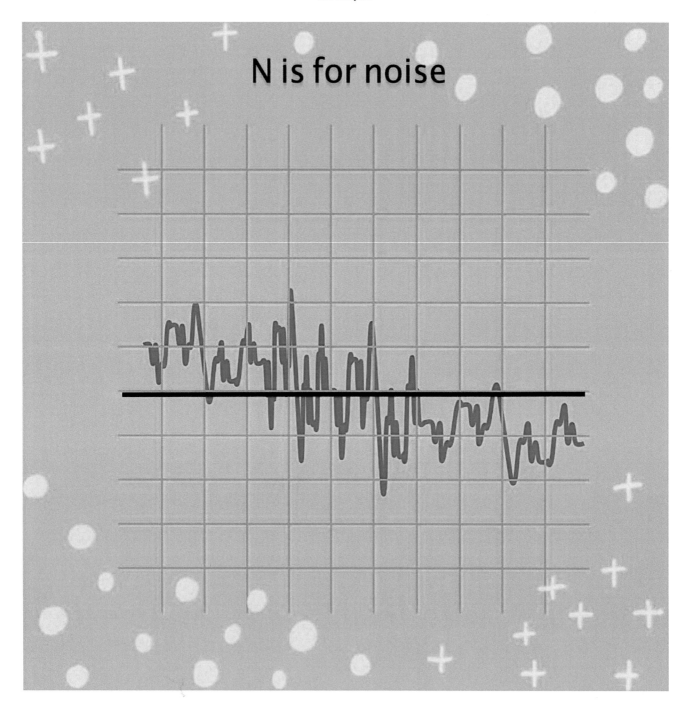

N is for noise

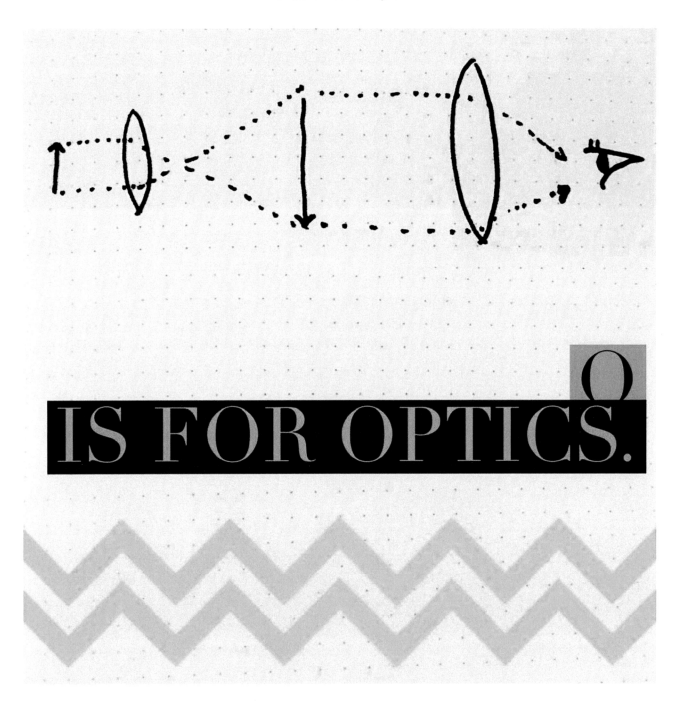

IS FOR OPTICS.

P IS FOR PHOTON

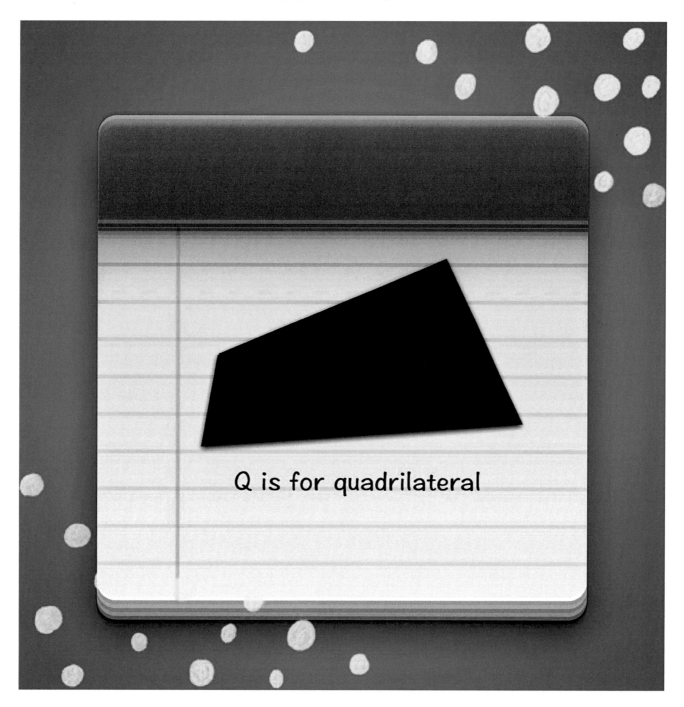

Q is for quadrilateral

R IS FOR

RESISTOR

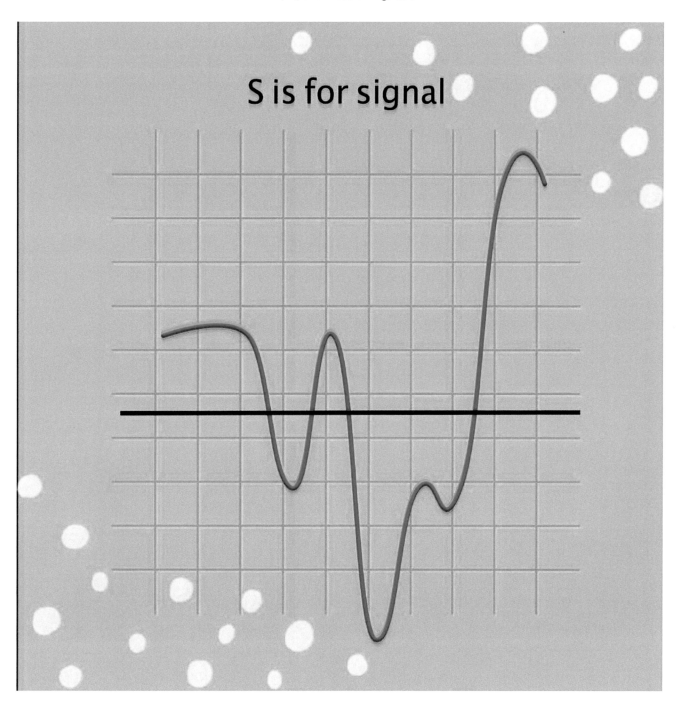

S is for signal

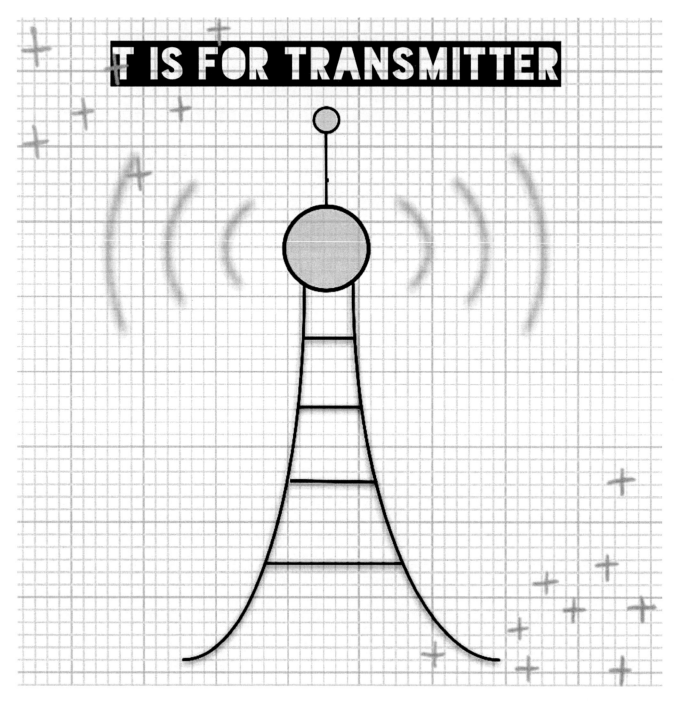

T IS FOR TRANSMITTER

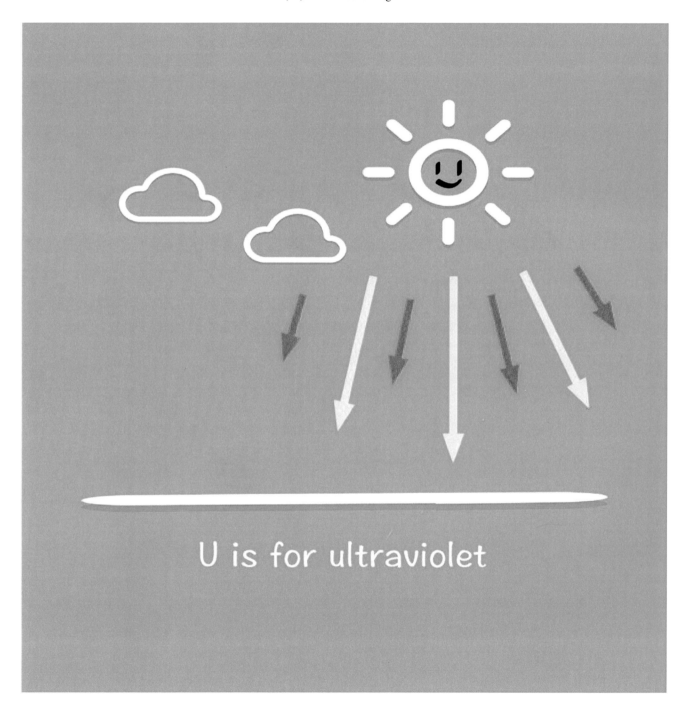

U is for ultraviolet

V is for voltage

W is for wave

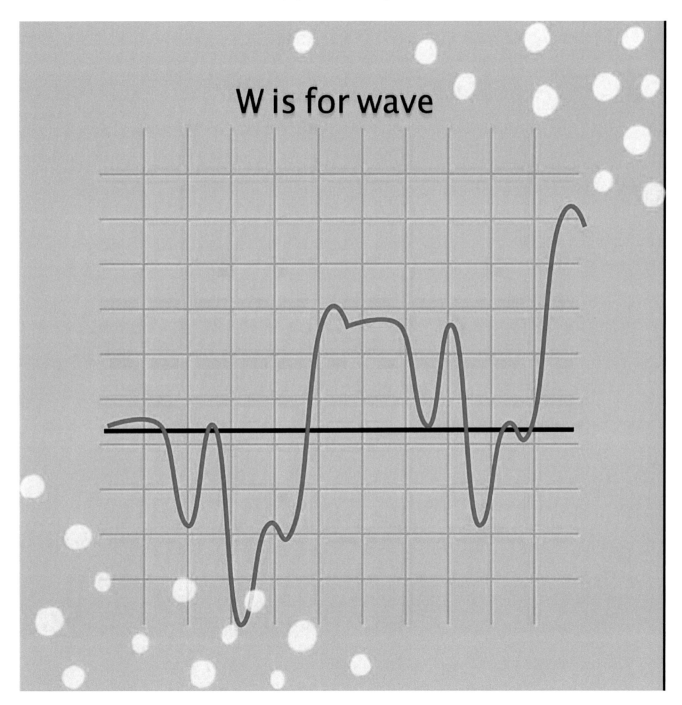

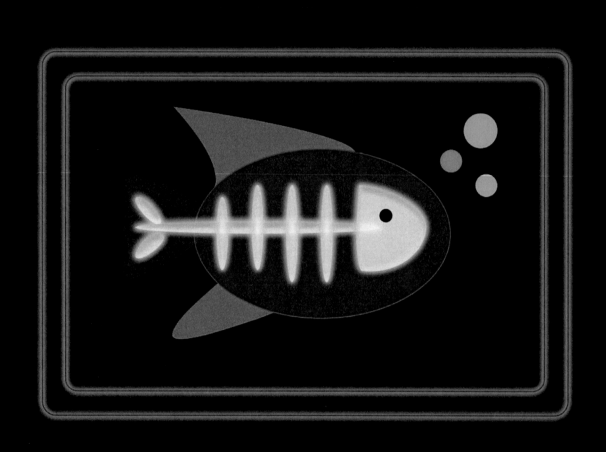

X is for x-ray

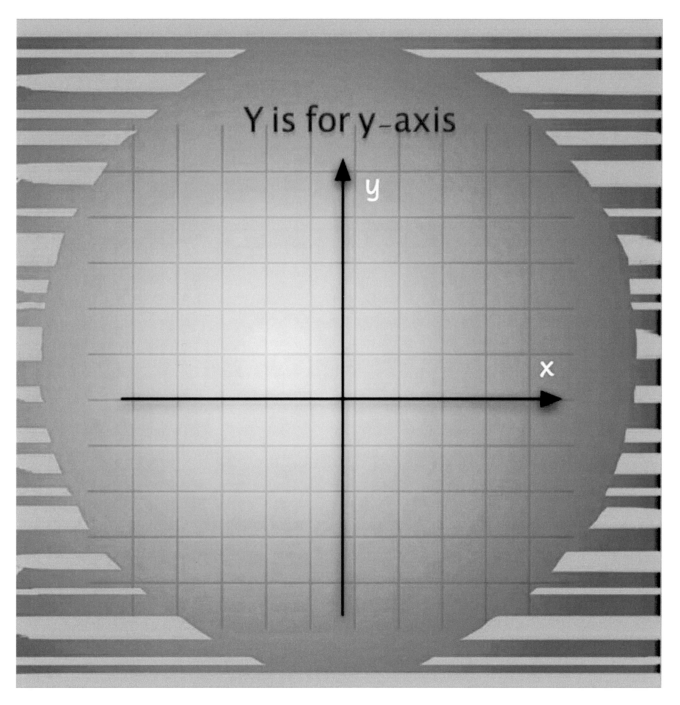

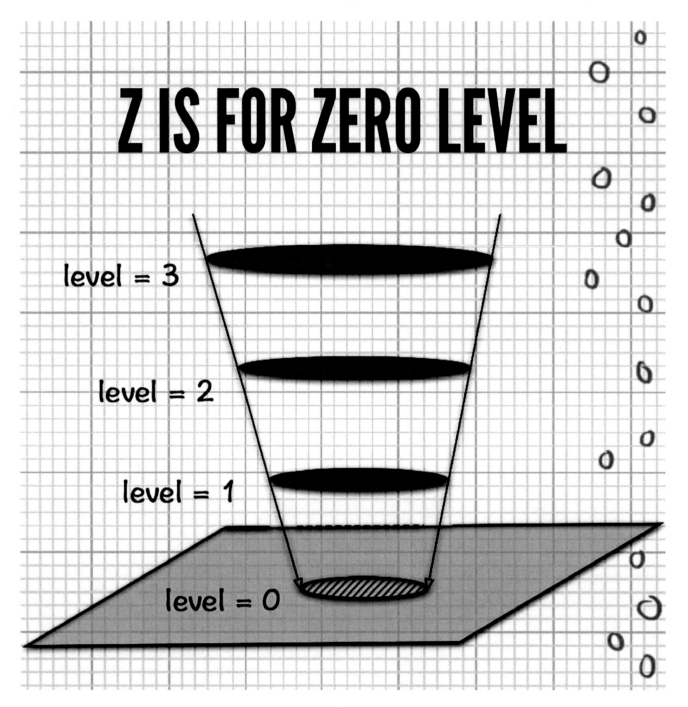

Jie Jacquot

ABOUT THE AUTHOR

Jie Zhu Jacquot likes numbers and laws of nature and has a Ph.D. in Electrical Engineering. She lives in Redondo Beach, CA with her husband and daughter and enjoys hiking, surfing, reading, deadpan comedy and indie movies.

Made in the USA
San Bernardino, CA
04 October 2015